D1515334

# SOUND AND LIGHT

## DAVID GLOVER

WITHDRAWN

Kingfisher Books

NEW YORK

KINGFISHER BOOKS
Larousse Kingfisher Chambers Inc.
95 Madison Avenue
New York, New York 10016

First American edition 1993
10 9 8 7 6 5 4 3 2 (HC)
10 9 8 7 6 5 4 3 (PB)
10 9 8 7 6 5 4 3 2 1 (LIB. BDG.)
© Grisewood & Dempsey Ltd. 1993

Library of Congress
Cataloging-in-Publication Data

Glover, David
    Sound and light / David Glover. —
1st American ed.
      p.  cm. — (Young discoverers)
    Includes index.
    Summary: Uses activities and
experiments to introduce the properties of
light and sound.
    1. Sound-waves — Juvenile literature.
2. Sound-waves — Experiments — Juvenile
literature.  3. Light — Juvenile literature.
4. Light — Experiments — Juvenile
literature.  [1. Sound — Experiments.
2. Light — Experiments.  3. Experiments.]
I. Title  II. Series.
QC243.2.G56 1993
534'.078 — dc20      92-40213 CIP AC

ISBN 1-85697-839-7 (HC)
ISBN 1-85697-935-0 (PB)
ISBN 1-85697-632-7 (LIB. BDG.)

Series editor: Sue Nicholson
Designer: Ben White
Author: David Glover
Photo research: Elaine Willis
Cover design: Dave West
Cover illustration: Kuo Kang Chen
Illustrators: Kuo Kang Chen pp.2, 9 (bot. right),
    10 (left), 12 (bot.), 19, 20 (bot.), 21 (top), 23,
    24-25, 26-27 (bot.), 30-31 (bot.); David Evans,
    Kathy Jakeman Illustration pp.10 (bot. right), 12
    (top), 26 (top); Chris Forsey pp.4-5, 6 (bot. left),
    8 (top right), 16 (bot.), 17, 21 (bot.); Hayward
    Art Group pp.16 (top and right), 18 (top right),
    27 (top), 28-29; Hussein Hussein pp.6 (right), 7,
    8 (bot. left), 9 (top); Kevin Maddison pp.7 (top
    right), 11, 13, 14-15, 18 (bot.), 20 (top), 22, 31
    (top)

Photographs: Hutchinson Library p.19; Kanehara
    Shuppan Co., Ltd. p.29; Life File Photo Library
    p.24, NHPA pp.17, 29, 30; ZEFA pp.5, 10, 13

Printed in Spain

# About This Book

This book tells you about sound and light — what they are and how we use them to hear and to see. It also suggests lots of experiments and things to look out for. Nearly everything you need to do the experiments can be found around the home. You may have to buy some items, but they are all cheap and easy to find. Sometimes you will need to ask an adult to help you, such as when heating up hot liquids or drilling holes.

**Be a Smart Scientist**
- Before you begin the experiments, read the instructions carefully and collect all the things you need.
- Put on some old clothes or a smock.
- When you have finished, clear everything away, especially sharp things like knives and scissors, and wash your hands.
- Keep a record of what you do and the things you find out.

If your results aren't quite the same as those in this book, don't worry. See if you can work out what has happened, and why.

# Contents

 Thunder and Lightning 4

 Sound Waves 6

 Feeling Sound 8

 Making Music 10

 Moving Sound 13

 Bouncing Sound 14

 How Do You Hear? 16

 Light Waves 18

 Light and Shade 20

 Look in the Mirror 22

 Amazing Mirrors 24

 Bending Light 25

 How Lenses Work 26

 How Do You See? 28

 Light of Many Colors 30

Index 32

# Thunder and Lightning

Have you ever been caught in a thunderstorm? First you see a flash of lightning, then you hear a crash of thunder. The sky is filled with light and sound.

Lightning flashes are huge sparks of electricity. They are so powerful they can be seen a long way from a storm. Light travels very fast, so we see the flash of light in the same second that it is made. But sound travels more slowly. It may be several seconds before the sound of a thunderclap reaches our ears.

The Vikings believed that thunder was the sound of their god, Odin, hammering his sword ready for war.

## How Far Is the Storm?

Light travels a million times faster than sound, so it arrives almost instantly. But sound takes about 5 seconds to travel 1 mile.

You can work out how far a thunderstorm is from you by timing the number of seconds between seeing a lightning flash and hearing the roll of thunder.

If you count $2\frac{1}{2}$ seconds, then the storm is half a mile away, 5 seconds means that it is 1 mile away, 10 seconds 2 miles, and so on.

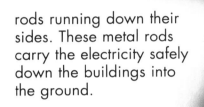

The giant sparks of electricity given off by lightning can strike tall trees and set them on fire. So **never** shelter under a tree during a thunderstorm.

In cities, many tall buildings have lightning rods running down their sides. These metal rods carry the electricity safely down the buildings into the ground.

5

# Sound Waves

If you flick the end of a rope up and down, the "flick" travels along the rope like a wave — the section of rope in your hand passes the movement on to the next section, which passes it on again, and so on. This is how sound travels through the air. When you burst a balloon, the escaping air gives a sudden push to the air around it. This push is passed on through the air like the wave traveling along the rope and we hear the loud bang, or pop, when the sound wave reaches our ears.

## Making a Bang

Bursting an air-filled paper bag forces the air trapped inside the bag through the hole in the paper. This sends a powerful sound wave through the air that reaches our ears as a loud bang.

Tie a rope to a tree or to a lamppost and flick the free end up and down to see how waves move along the rope.

## Passing It On

Set up a row of dominoes, spacing them fairly close together. Now knock the first one over and watch how the wave travels down the line.

6

# Do it yourself

**Build a sound cannon so you can see a sound wave make a candle flicker. You will need a cardboard tube, some plastic, scissors, tape, a small candle, a saucer, and some sand.**

**1.** Stretch the pieces of plastic tightly across each end of the cardboard tube and tape them firmly in place.

**2.** Make a small hole in the middle of the plastic at one end of the tube.

tape firmly in place or use rubber bands

plastic cut from plastic bag

**3.** Put some sand in the saucer and stand the candle upright in it. Ask an adult to light the candle for you.

**4.** Hold the end of the tube with the hole in it about an inch away from the flame.

## Noisiest Explosion

When the Indonesian island of Krakatoa exploded in 1883, the sound wave was heard in Australia, 2,500 miles away.

**5.** Tap the other end of the tube with your finger. Watch what happens to the flame.

## How It Works

When you tap the plastic, you make a sound wave that travels down the tube and out of the hole at the end. The wave can be strong enough to blow out the candle flame.

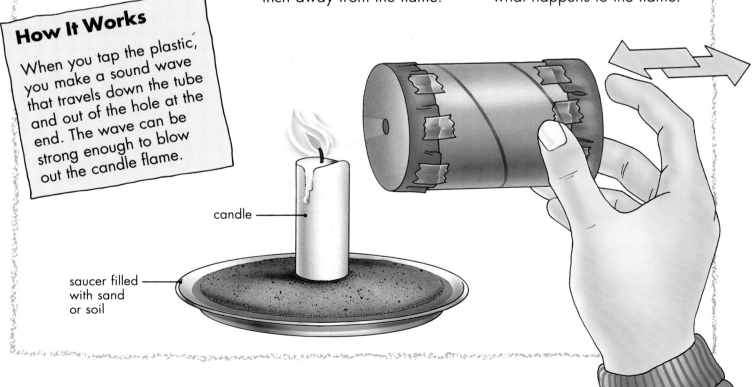

candle

saucer filled with sand or soil

# Feeling Sound

If you bend the end of a ruler over the edge of a table and then let it go, the ruler will move up and down. When something moves quickly back and forth like this, we say that it is vibrating.

Try changing the length of the ruler on the table. The shorter the length over the edge, the quicker the vibrations and the higher the sound. We call the number of sound waves a second, the *frequency* of the waves.

Nearly every sound you hear is made by something vibrating.

## Feeling Vibrations

When something is making a steady sound it must be vibrating to push the air around it back and forth. If you hold your hand against things making sounds you can usually feel the vibrations. Here are some things to test:
- a purring cat
- a ringing telephone
- your throat when you are singing
- a radio playing loud music

## Seeing Vibrations

We cannot see sound waves, but sometimes we can see the vibrations that make sounds. Sprinkle a few grains of uncooked rice on some paper, lay it over a radio and watch the rice jump!

turn up sound

press this end down firmly

8

If you stretch a rubber band between your fingers and twang it, it vibrates and makes a quiet sound. The sound isn't very loud because the band is small and it can only push a small amount of air. To make the sound louder we must amplify it. In other words, we must make the vibrations of the elastic band push more air to and fro.

# Do it yourself

**Make a sound amplifier. You will need a large plastic mixing bowl, a sheet of plastic cut from a plastic bag, tape, scissors, and two rubber bands.**

**1.** Stretch the plastic tightly over the top of the bowl, like the skin of a drum. Secure the plastic with a rubber band and tape.

**2.** Tape the other rubber band to the middle of the plastic.

**3.** Now stretch the loose band and twang it.

## How It Works

When the band vibrates it makes the stretched plastic vibrate. Because the plastic sheet is much bigger than the elastic band, it pushes a lot more air and amplifies the sound. That's why a jackhammer makes a very loud noise — it vibrates the ground around it.

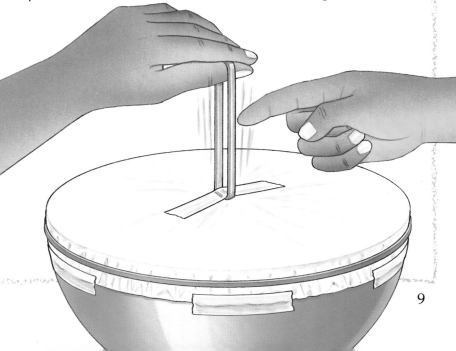

9

# Making Music

All musical instruments use vibrations to make sounds. Stringed instruments, like guitars, have stretched strings that vibrate when they are plucked or strummed. Wind instruments, like recorders or clarinets, make vibrations when the musician blows down the tube. Percussion instruments, like drums, triangles, and cymbals, are usually played by hitting or tapping them to make them vibrate.

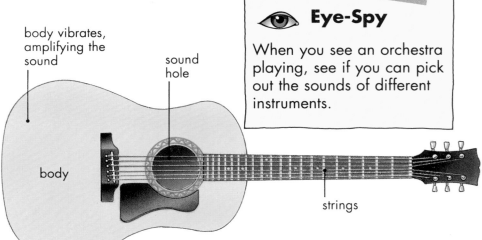

## 👁 Eye-Spy

When you see an orchestra playing, see if you can pick out the sounds of different instruments.

## Moving Air

Because a triangle only moves a small amount of air, it makes a quiet sound. The cymbals are bigger and move a lot more air. So they make a loud sound when they are crashed together.

triangle

cymbals

body vibrates, amplifying the sound

sound hole

body

strings

funnel-shape amplifies the sound

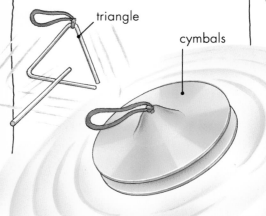

The trumpet is a brass instrument. The player makes sounds by vibrating her lips.

# Do it yourself

## Make your own musical instruments.

**1.** Make a trumpet with a short piece of hose and a funnel. When you blow into it, try to vibrate your lips — it takes lots of practice to get a clear note.

**2.** Try blowing over the top of an empty bottle. If you fill several bottles with different amounts of water, you can get high and low notes. Or you could blow sharply over a pen top to make a high, piercing whistle.

**3.** Make a rich, deep note with a string bass like the one in the picture. Ask an adult to drill a hole in one end of the pole so you can thread string through it. Knot the string tightly under the top of the box and pluck it. Cut a hole in the box to make the sound louder.

**4.** Tap small cans, large pans, big, empty boxes, or glass jars with pens, spoons, or anything else you can find. Some things will make dull sounds that fade quickly. Others vibrate for longer and make bright sounds that ring on.

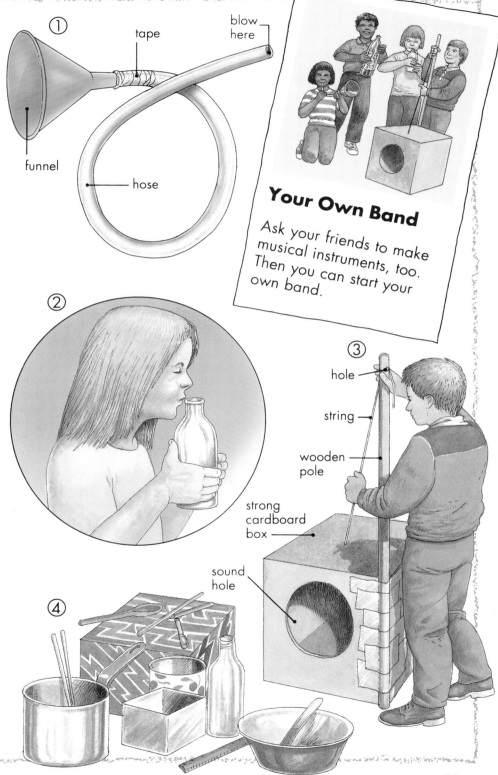

① tape — blow here — funnel — hose

## Your Own Band

Ask your friends to make musical instruments, too. Then you can start your own band.

②

③ hole — string — wooden pole — strong cardboard box — sound hole

④

11

## Finding the Right Note

Bass drums and tubas make low notes like the rumble of a large truck or the growl of a bear. Small, light instruments, such as triangles and whistles, produce high notes like the sounds made by mice or small birds.

Violin players can make both high and low notes by pressing the violin's strings with their fingers. When the vibrating part of the string is made shorter, it vibrates more quickly and produces a higher note.

A violin player makes the strings vibrate by scraping them with a bow.

# Do it yourself

**Make a set of musical pipes with plastic straws, thick cardboard, and tape.**

**1.** Ask an adult to soften the ends of the straws in very hot water. Flatten the ends of the straws and cut each of the ends to a point, as shown on the right.

**2.** Now cut the straws to different lengths and tape them to the cardboard.

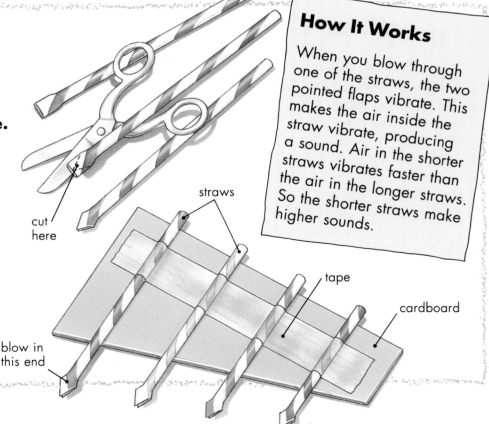

cut here

straws

tape

cardboard

blow in this end

## How It Works

When you blow through one of the straws, the two pointed flaps vibrate. This makes the air inside the straw vibrate, producing a sound. Air in the shorter straws vibrates faster than the air in the longer straws. So the shorter straws make higher sounds.

# Moving Sound

Sound can travel through other things besides air. Test this out by asking a friend to tap some metal railings with a stick while you stand farther down the railings. You should be able to hear the sound, but if you put your ear close to the metal the sound will be a lot louder.

Sound also travels well through water. In fact, sound travels five times faster through water than it does through air.

 **Eye-Spy**

Next time you swim in the ocean or a pool, listen to how different everything sounds underwater. (Only try this if you can swim really well!)

## Do it yourself

**Make a yogurt container telephone to hear sounds travel along string.**

string (about 10 feet long)

yogurt container

knot

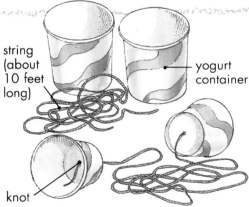

**1.** Ask an adult to help you make a small hole in the bottom of each container.

**2.** Thread the ends of the string through each hole and knot them. Hold one of the containers to your ear while a friend speaks into the other. Remember to keep the string tightly stretched.

## How It Works

Your friend's voice makes the bottom of his or her container vibrate. This makes the string vibrate, too. The sound waves travel along the string, making the bottom of your container vibrate so that you hear your friend's voice.

# Bouncing Sound

If you shout when you are standing in a tunnel or in a large, empty room, the sound made by your voice will hit the walls and bounce back. This reflected sound is called an echo. Echoes are louder when they hit a hard barrier, like the walls of a tunnel. Soft materials, like carpets and drapes, absorb or soak up sound. That's why you will hear an echo in an empty room but will not in one that is full of furniture.

## Making Echoes

Good places to experiment with echoes are near high cliffs or under bridges.

If you face a cliff and shout loudly, the sound waves will hit the hard rock and bounce back. You may even hear several echoes if the sound is reflected from different parts of the cliff.

Echoes made under bridges are louder than ones made by a cliff because the sounds have no room to spread out.

## Animal Echoes

Bats find food by making high-pitched squeaks and then listening for the echoes from insects. Dolphins use echoes to find food, too.

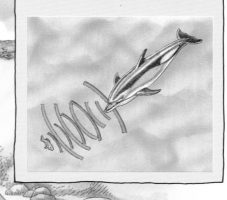

echo

sound

echo

14

# Do it yourself

**Test different materials to find out which ones are better at reflecting sound.**

**1.** Set up the experiment as shown in the picture. Make sure that the cardboard tubes do not touch and that they are about 2 inches from the material to be tested.

**2.** Move the listening tube to catch the sound.

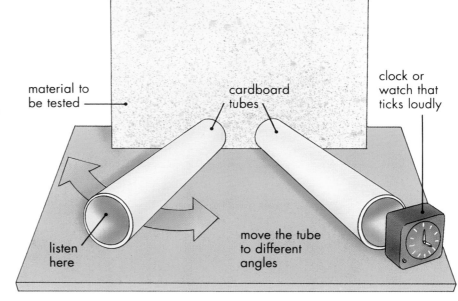

material to be tested

cardboard tubes

clock or watch that ticks loudly

listen here

move the tube to different angles

paper

cloth

metal

**3.** Try listening for the reflected sound of the clock's tick against the wall first. Then you could try paper, cloth, a metal tray, a mirror, and a cushion. Which materials reflect the sound best? Which absorb it?

## How It Works

The strongest reflection comes from hard, smooth materials like metal or glass. The sound bounces off the materials at the same angle that it strikes — like a ball bouncing off a smooth floor.

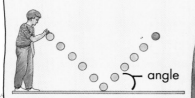

angle

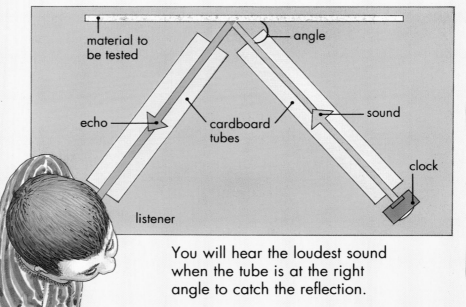

material to be tested

angle

echo

cardboard tubes

sound

clock

listener

You will hear the loudest sound when the tube is at the right angle to catch the reflection.

# How Do You Hear?

The drawing below shows what the inside of your ear looks like. The part outside your head catches sounds. Inside, there is a small piece of skin stretched tight like the skin on a drum. This is called the eardrum. When sounds enter your ear, they make the eardrum vibrate. The vibrations are amplified and are picked up by nerves. The nerves then send signals about the sound to your brain and you "hear."

hearing aid

## Hearing Aids

Some people can't hear very well because their ears have been damaged. Hearing aids are tiny electrical amplifiers that pick up and amplify sounds as they enter the ear.

## How Loud is Loud?

The loudness of a sound is measured in decibels (dB for short). Sounds over 100 dB can damage your ears.
- Airplane 100-150 dB
- Jackhammer 100 dB
- Loud music 90-95dB
- Talking 40-60 dB
- Whispering 20 dB
- Falling leaves 10 dB

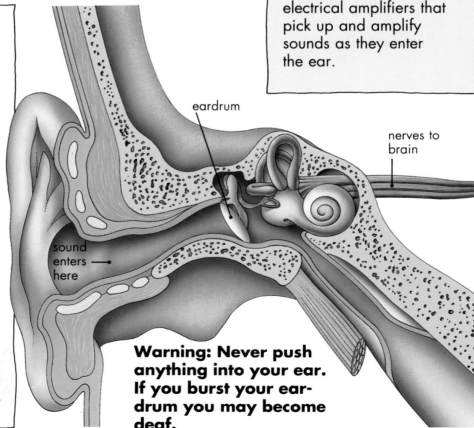

eardrum

nerves to brain

sound enters here

earmuffs to protect ears

**Warning: Never push anything into your ear. If you burst your eardrum you may become deaf.**

# Do it yourself

## Can you tell which direction sounds are coming from?

**1.** Put on a blindfold and ask a friend to make a sound, sometimes from behind you and sometimes to the right or left.

**2.** Try pointing in the direction of the sound each time. You could experiment with different sounds (like humming) and distances.

whistle

point at direction sound is coming from

blindfold

**3.** Try blocking one ear. Does this make it easier or more difficult to tell the direction of the sound?

## 👁 Eye-Spy

Watch for animals using their ears. Hares can twist their long ears around so they can check where a sound is coming from. Sometimes you can see birds tilting their heads toward sounds, too.

# Light Waves

Without light from the Sun, the Earth would be a dark, cold, lifeless place. Light is a kind of energy. We use light to see. Plants use it to grow.

Like sound, light travels in waves. But light does not need to travel through air or water. It can pass through empty space where there is no air or water to carry it. Light waves travel in straight lines, but they travel so fast we can't see them move. We just see a straight, steady beam of light.

## First Light Bulb

The first electric light was invented by Thomas Edison in 1879. He used electricity to heat a piece of burnt thread so it glowed brightly.

## Light All Around

We need light to be able to see. During the day, we get light from the Sun. At night, or in a dark room, we use artificial light, such as light from electric light bulbs.

When you read a book by sunlight or by lamplight, the light is reflected from the pages of the book into your eyes. Different things reflect different amounts of light. That is why some things look shiny and bright and others look dull.

# Do it yourself

**See for yourself how light travels in straight lines. You will need a bright flashlight and some cardboard.**

**1.** Cut out three pieces of cardboard the same size and make a small hole in the center of each of them.

## Straight Beams

Sometimes, rays of sunlight are broken up by trees or clouds. You can then see that the light rays are straight.

**2.** Line up the cards so you can see the light shining through the holes. (You could support them in modeling clay or ask a friend to help.)

**3.** Now move the middle card from side to side. You will only be able to see the light when the three holes are in a straight line.

look here

# Light and Shade

Some things, like glass and water, are transparent. This means that light can pass through them. Other things, like metal and stone, are opaque. They block out the light. As light travels in straight lines it cannot bend around opaque objects, so these things cast shadows. The middle part of a shadow is very dark. It is called the umbra. The lighter edge is called the penumbra.

## Blocking the Sun

Light passes through the transparent glass of the window so we can see through it. But the shade is opaque and blocks out the Sun's light.

## Do it yourself

### See how shadows work.

Put a piece of white paper on a table under a bright lamp. Hold a small piece of thick cardboard or a coaster in front of the light to make a shadow. Try moving the cardboard toward and away from the light to see the how the shadow's shape changes.

### Fly's Eye View

If a fly sat in the middle of the umbra, it would see a dark circle blocking out the light. A fly on the penumbra would see part of the light shining past the cardboard.

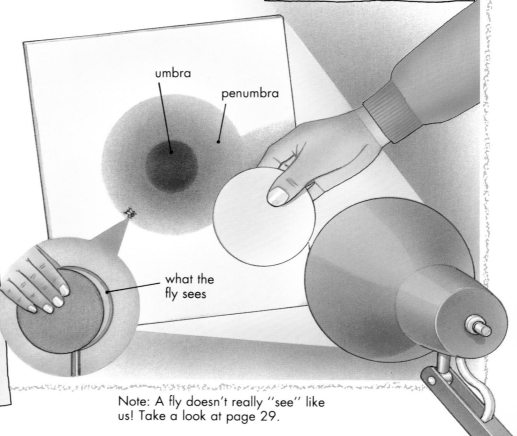

umbra

penumbra

what the fly sees

Note: A fly doesn't really "see" like us! Take a look at page 29.

## Shadows in Space

When the Moon passes between the Sun and the Earth it blocks out the Sun's light and casts a shadow on the Earth. This is called an eclipse of the Sun.

Where the middle of the Moon's shadow (the umbra) falls on Earth there is a total eclipse of the Sun. Where the edge of its shadow falls on Earth there is a partial eclipse of the Sun.

total eclipse— as seen from the umbra

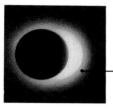

partial eclipse— as seen from the penumbra

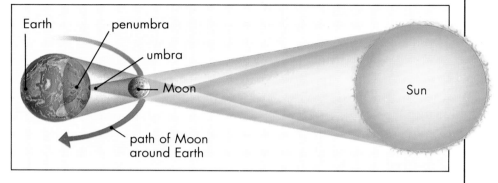

Earth

penumbra

umbra

Moon

Sun

path of Moon around Earth

# Do it yourself

**Your own body is opaque — that's why you have a shadow. Why not set up a shadow screen and play some shadow games.**

Use a good, bright light, such as a slide projector. Hang up a white sheet for your screen. Stand close to the sheet to cast a dark, clear shadow.

### Things to Try

- Guess an object from its shadow's shape.
- Draw around shadows made by people's faces to make silhouettes.
- Make shadow puppets and put on a play.

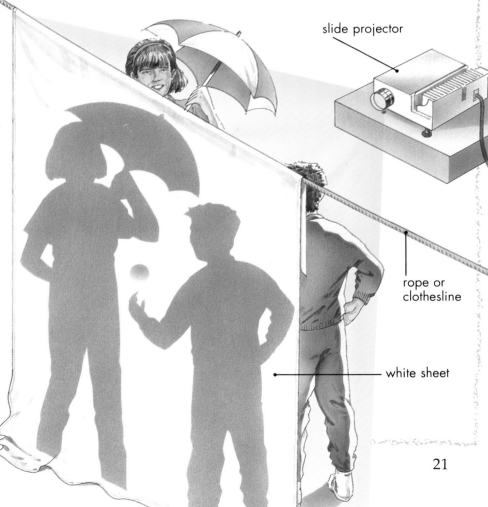

slide projector

rope or clothesline

white sheet

21

# Look in the Mirror

When light hits a surface, the light rays are reflected, or bounced back. Flat, shiny surfaces reflect light best. That's why mirrors are made of flat, highly polished glass with a shiny silver coating on the back. When you look in a mirror you can see a reflection of yourself. Mirrors can be used to change the direction of light to see into awkward spots — like a dentist looking at your back teeth!

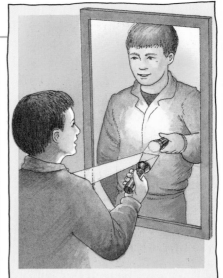

### 👁 Eye-Spy

If you shine a flashlight into a mirror you can see how the mirror reflects the beam of light.

## Do it yourself

**Find one or two small mirrors and try these different ways of reflecting light.**

**1.** Can you read the numbers? You could practice mirror writing and send secret messages to your friends.

① 

place mirror — on blue line

**2.** Catch the Sun's light and send signals.

**3.** See around corners.

**4.** Make kaleidoscope patterns. (Place a mirror on each line.)

④

③

Note: Never look directly at the Sun, even when it is reflected in a mirror.

# Do it yourself

**Make a periscope to look over the heads of a crowd of people or to peep over a wall.**

**1.** Cut out two holes of the same size at the top and bottom of an empty juice or milk carton. One hole must be on each side.

**2.** Measure and draw two squares on both sides of each hole and divide the squares with diagonal lines. This is to help you make sure that the mirrors are at the same angle of 45°. Ask an adult to help.

**3.** Cut out two diagonal slits on each side, as shown. They should be just big enough to slide your mirrors through.

**4.** Slip the mirrors in place with the reflecting sides facing each other.

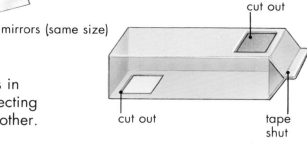

cardboard carton

mirrors (same size)

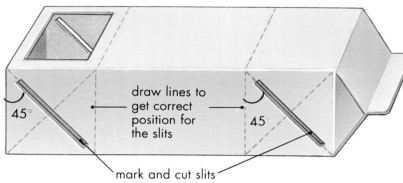

cut out

cut out

tape shut

45°

45

draw lines to get correct position for the slits

mark and cut slits

The picture below shows how the mirrors change the direction of light. Light hits the top mirror and is reflected down to the bottom mirror and then into your eyes.

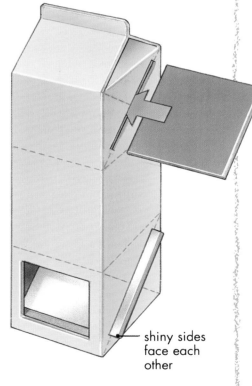

shiny sides face each other

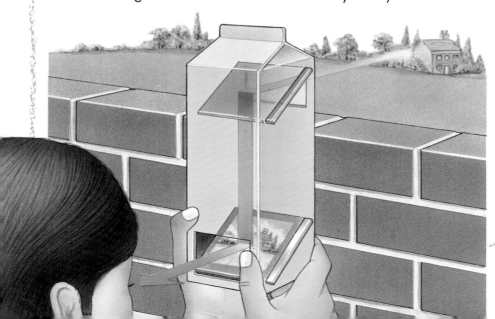

23

# Amazing Mirrors

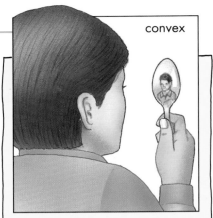
convex

Many mirrors are flat, but some are curved. A concave mirror curves down in the middle. If you stand close to a concave mirror it magnifies you, so you look bigger. If you stand farther away, your reflection will be upside down. A convex mirror curves up in the middle. It makes you look smaller but you can see more behind.

 **Eye-Spy**

Look at your reflection in a bright, shiny spoon. In the convex side, you look smaller but you can see a lot of the room behind you. In the concave side, your image will be big if you hold the spoon close but smaller and upside down if you hold it farther away.

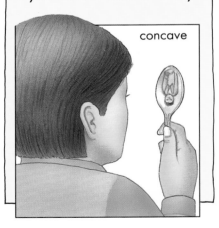
concave

Curved mirrors can be fun! They reflect the light in different directions so your reflection can look stretched, squashed, or twisted.

# Bending Light

A straight straw in a glass of water looks bent. This is because light travels more slowly through water than it does through air, and when light slows down it can also change direction. This is called refraction. Glass refracts light, too. Look at some stamps through the bottom of a thick glass and see how their shape changes.

## Do it yourself

**Test refraction with this magic coin trick. You will need a glass, a coin, a marker, and some water.**

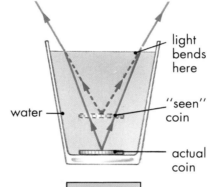

light bends here

water

"seen" coin

actual coin

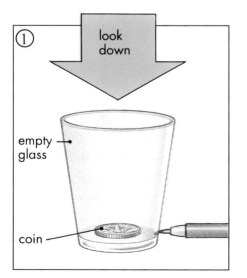

① look down

empty glass

coin

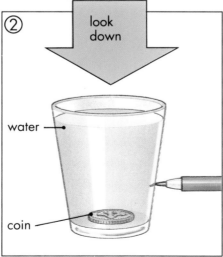

② look down

water

coin

**1.** Put a coin in the bottom of an empty glass. Look down into the glass and, at the same time, lower the marker along the side until you think it is at the same height as the coin. Were you right?

**2.** Now fill the glass with water and try the experiment again. You will probably find that you do not lower your marker far enough. This is because refraction makes the water look shallower than it really is.

25

# How Lenses Work

Lenses are pieces of glass or clear plastic that are specially curved to bend light by refraction. If you look through a concave lens, things look smaller. Convex lenses can make things look bigger. Magnifying glasses and microscopes have convex lenses.

The lenses in eyeglasses help people see more clearly. We say that people who wear glasses with concave lenses are near-sighted, and people who wear glasses with convex lenses are farsighted.

## 👁 Eye-Spy

Do you or your friends wear glasses? Are the glasses concave or convex? The box on the next page tells you how to test them.

## Do it yourself

**Make a simple magnifier to make things look bigger.**

**1.** Cut a hole in a piece of cardboard or use a slide mount.

clear tape

**2.** Cover the hole with clear plastic tape and use a pencil to drip a single drop of water over it. The rounded droplet should magnify things slightly.

You could also try looking at things through the bottom of a thick glass or a glass filled with water.

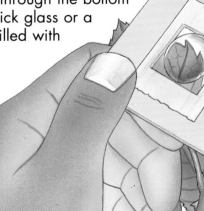

## Testing Lenses

Collect some old pairs of glasses. First, look at some print in a book. If the words look smaller, the lenses are concave. If they look bigger, the lenses are convex.

Another test for lenses is to look at the shadows they cast on a sheet of paper. Concave lenses spread the light so they cast a big, dark shadow. Convex lenses concentrate the light. Their shadow is small and bright.

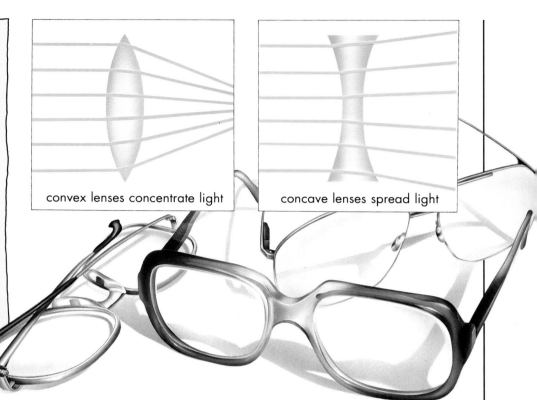

convex lenses concentrate light

concave lenses spread light

# Do it yourself

**Try this experiment with a convex lens from an old pair of reading glasses or a magnifying glass to see how it concentrates light.**

Stand opposite a sunny window and move your lens toward a sheet of white paper until you can see an image of the window and the scene outside. The image will be upside down. The lenses in your eyes work in a similar way. Look at the box at the bottom of the next page.

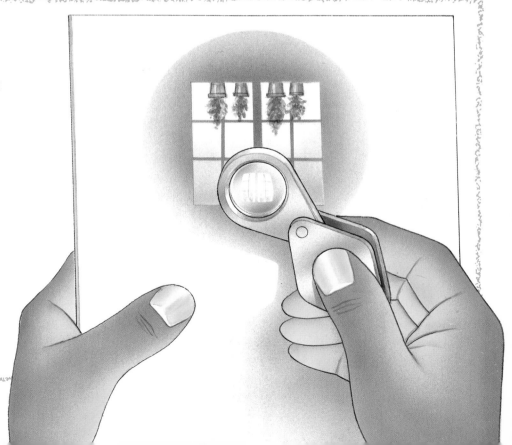

# How Do You See?

Look at your eyes in a mirror. The black spot in the middle is called the pupil. The colored part around the pupil is the iris. The size of the iris changes to make the pupil bigger or smaller. In very bright light the pupil gets smaller so you are not dazzled. In dim light the pupil gets larger to let more light into your eye. If you go into a dark room after being in strong sunlight you can't see much at first. But after a while your eyes adjust and you can see more clearly.

iris      pupil

## Looking at Eyes

Look at your eyes in a mirror. Close them. Count to 20. Open your eyes. Your pupils will be larger to let in more light.

## How Eyes Work

The lens collects the light that enters your eye and focuses a small picture onto the retina at the back of your eye. (This works in a similar way to the lens you used in the activity on page 27.) The retina sends messages about the picture to your brain. The brain sorts out the image so it looks the right way up, and you can make sense of what you see.

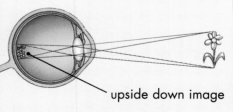

upside down image

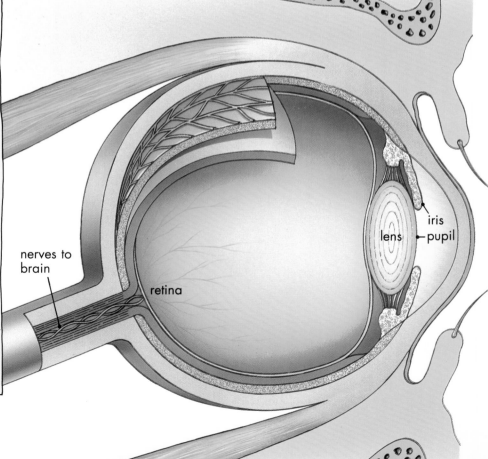

nerves to brain

retina

lens

iris
pupil

## Seeing in the Dark

Owls and cats hunt for food at night. Owls have large pupils to collect as much light as possible.

During the day, a cat's pupils are narrow slits, but at night they become wider to let in more light.

day          night

## Seeing all Around

A fly has large, dome-shaped eyes. Each eye is made up of thousands of tiny lenses and no two lenses point in the same direction. A fly can therefore see danger coming from most directions — it's almost impossible to sneak up on a fly!

##  Eye-Spy

Some people are color blind. This means that they cannot tell the difference between different colors.

For example, someone who cannot tell the difference between red and green may not be able to see the correct numbers in the circles on the right. People with normal sight read the top number as 5 and the bottom one as 8. Those with red-green color blindness may read the numbers as 2 and 3. A few people are completely color blind. They see everything in just black, white, and gray.

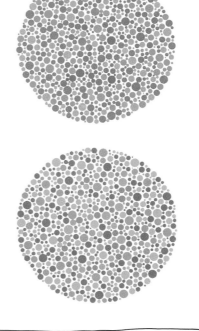

# Light of Many Colors

Although sunlight looks white, it is really made up of different colors. You can sometimes see these colors when sunlight passes through glass or water. The glass or water bends the colors by different amounts, and this makes them spread out in a rainbow pattern which we call the spectrum.

If it rains when the Sun is shining, the raindrops in the air sometimes separate the colors of sunlight and you see a rainbow in the sky.

## Rainbow Colors

A rainbow has all the colors of the spectrum — red, orange, yellow, green, blue, indigo, and violet.

## Do it yourself

**Here are some different ways of making your own rainbows.**

Lay a mirror at an angle in a dish of water. Stand the dish in front of a sunny window so that the light travels into the water and is reflected from the mirror onto some cardboard. The water covering the mirror should split the sunlight into the colors of the spectrum.

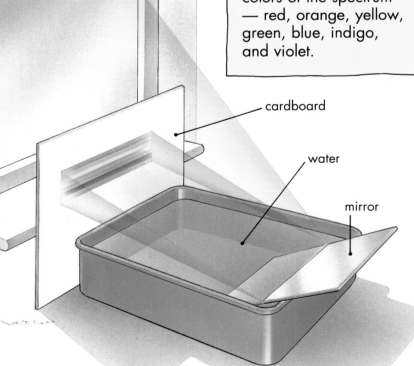

cardboard

water

mirror

## Seeing Colors

Most things do not make light of their own. They reflect light. The colors we see depend on which colors are reflected into our eyes. So a red flower looks red because it reflects more of the red part of the spectrum into our eyes than the other colors.

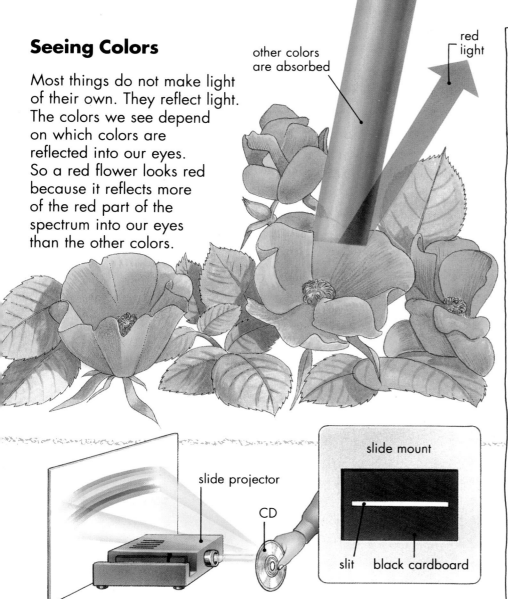

other colors are absorbed

red light

## Changing Colors

Look at the world through different colors. Shine a flashlight through colored candy wrappers, look through dyed water (food coloring works well), or buy colored light bulbs. These all filter light — a green filter only filters (lets through) green light.

slide projector

CD

slide mount

slit    black cardboard

If you hold a compact disc in front of a slide projector, you can cast lovely rainbow patterns onto white cardboard or a wall. This works best if you put a black slide with a narrow slit in it into the projector. Make one by putting two pieces of black cardboard into a slide mount. (Ask an adult to help.)

Or you could try just looking at a CD under bright light. The fine grooves in the CD reflect the light, splitting the colors into a spectrum.

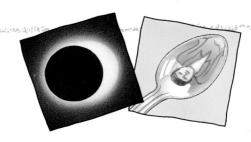
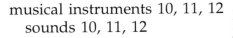

# Index

amplifier 16

color blindness 29
color 30, 31
compact disc 30, 31
concave, lens 26, 27
    mirror 24
convex, lens 26, 27
    mirror 24
decibel 16
drum 10

ears 16
eardrum 16

echo 14-15
eclipse 21
electricity 5
eyes 28-29

farsightedness 26

glasses 26, 27
guitar 10

hearing aid 16

iris 28

lens 26-27, 28
light, color of 30, 31
    speed of 4, 25
light waves 18
lightning 4, 5

magnifying glass 26
mirror 22-23, 24
Moon 21

musical instruments 10, 11, 12
    sounds 10, 11, 12

nearsightedness 26

opaque 20

penumbra 20
percussion instruments 10
pipes, musical 12
pupil 28

rainbow 30, 31
reflection of light 18, 22, 24
    of sound 14-15
refraction 25
retina 28

shadows 20, 21
sound, speed of 4, 13
sound waves 6-7, 8, 14
spectrum, color 30
string instruments 10
Sun 18, 19, 20

thunder 4
thunderstorm 4, 5
transparent objects 20
triangle 10
trumpet 10

umbra 20
underwater sound 13

vibration 8, 9
violin 12